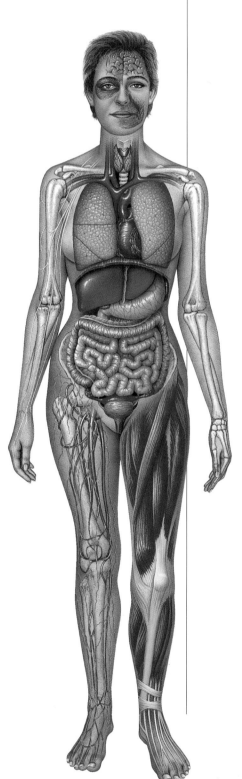

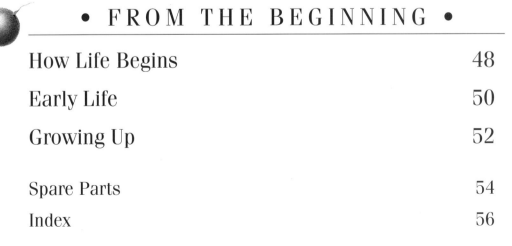

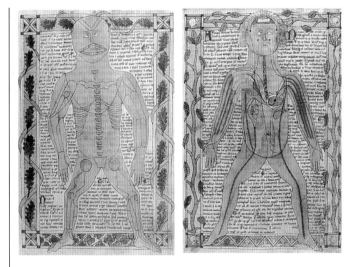

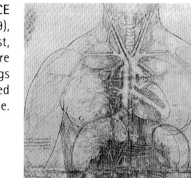

ROME'S MASTER PHYSICIAN
Claudius Galen (129-199) wrote more than 500 books on the human body. The Romans believed it was wrong to cut open human corpses, so Galen dissected animals and studied the wounds of gladiators.

• EVERY BODY TELLS A STORY •

In the Beginning

Our knowledge about the human body began long ago. Fossil remains of prehistoric people from 50,000 years ago show that they tried to heal broken bones by setting them in their natural positions. Ancient Egyptians carefully preserved the bodies of pharaohs with a technique called mummification. Ancient Chinese inserted needles into the body to balance life energy called chi. This procedure, called acupuncture, is still used in Chinese medicine. Ancient Greeks, such as Hippocrates, used their knowledge of the body to treat disease and illness. Ancient Romans studied the bodies of slaves and gladiators who had been injured in battles. The teachings of Rome's great physician Claudius Galen were followed for 1,200 years. When the Renaissance began in Europe in the 1300s, artists and scientists began to cast off old beliefs. By the 1500s, people understood much more about what really happened inside the human body.

OPEN TO VIEW
During the Renaissance, students in European universities and medical schools began to study body structure, or anatomy. In Padua, Italy, Andreas Vesalius founded the modern science of anatomy.

BODY ENERGY
The Chinese believe that a life energy flows along body channels, or meridians. If the flow is disturbed, a person becomes ill. The Chinese use acupuncture points to rebalance the energy flow and make the person well again.

The Human Body

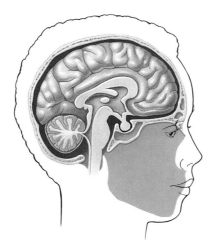

ISBN 1-74089-370-0
Colour reproduction by
Colourscan Overseas Co Pte Ltd
Printed by SNP Leefung Printers

Printed in China

The Human Body

CONSULTING EDITOR

Dr Marie Rose
Medical Practitioner
Sydney, Australia

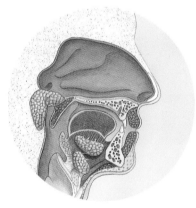

WELDON OWEN

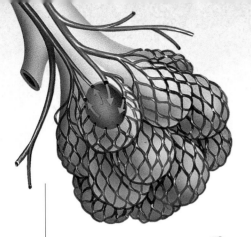

Contents

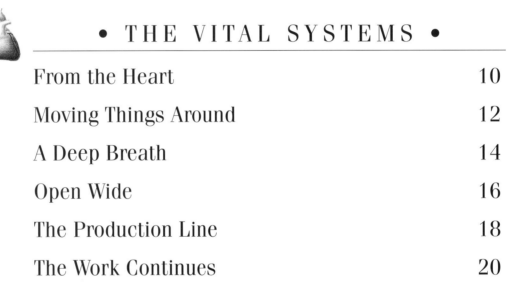

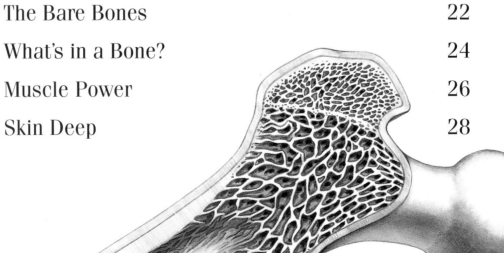

BODY WORSHIP

The Venus of Willendorf is a statue from the Stone Age. The statue is an example of how people have been fascinated with the shape of the human body for centuries.

THE REAL PICTURE

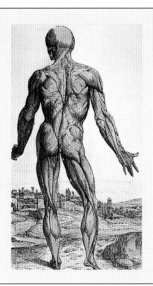

Andreas Vesalius was born in Brussels in 1514. When he was 24, he became a professor of anatomy at the University of Padua, Italy. He studied many human corpses, and sometimes hid them in his room for weeks. In 1543, he published a book called *De Humani Corporis Fabrica* (On the Structure of the Human Body). It contained detailed drawings of bodies, such as the one on the right, and caused huge arguments because it went against the teachings of Galen, Aristotle and others. Vesalius drew exactly what he saw and suggested how body parts worked together. His work was the beginning of modern scientific anatomy.

LOOKING AT CELLS
Early microscopes could magnify cells only up to 100 times. This soon improved to 2,000 times, which revealed many kinds of tiny cells inside the body.

GETTING SMALLER
Electron microscopes use electron beams instead of light beams. They make things look a million times bigger, so they can show the tiniest parts of a single cell.

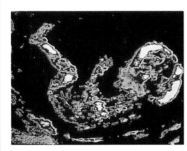

USING SOUND
Ultrasound scans, developed in the 1950s, beam very high-pitched sound waves into the body and detect the echoes. The echoes are converted into a picture. Ultrasounds are used to check a baby's progress in the womb.

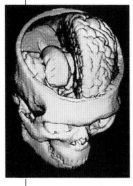

A HEAD IN 3-D
In the 1960s, the CT (Computerised Tomography) scan was the first to show three-dimensional images of body parts. It uses a very weak X-ray beam.

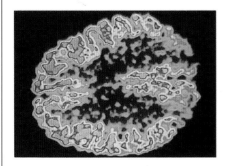

VIEWING THE BRAIN
The PET (Positron Emission Tomography) scan reveals how much energy a body part is using. It shows which areas of the brain are busiest when a person is doing a particular activity.

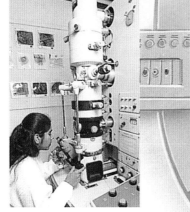

• EVERY BODY TELLS A STORY •

The Story So Far

In the fourteenth century, scientists began to question traditional knowledge and teachings. They began to study the body in two main ways. The first, called anatomy, looks at how the body is made—its shape and structure. The second, called physiology, tests how the body works—what the parts do, and how they function together. New inventions and discoveries revealed more about the body's anatomy and physiology. The microscope, invented about 1608, showed that the body was made up of billions of cells. X-rays, discovered in 1895, allowed doctors to see inside the body without cutting it open. Scanners were invented in the twentieth century with the help of computer technology. These allow images of the inside of the human body to be processed and viewed on a computer or television screen.

SLICES OF THE BODY

Magnetic Resonance Imaging (MRI) was invented in the 1970s. The MRI scanner shows details of soft tissues, such as muscles, nerves and blood vessels, by capturing images in sections, or "slices", of the body. A computer then builds up a picture of the body.

AMAZING IMAGES

In 1895, German scientist Wilhelm Röntgen discovered X-rays. As he experimented with high-voltage electrical equipment, he noticed that it gave off mysterious rays that passed through skin but not through bone. He could see the body's skeleton clearly. Within weeks, doctors were using X-rays to check injured people for broken bones.

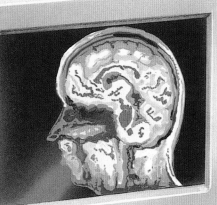

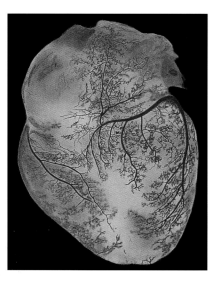

BRANCHES OF BLOOD
The thick, muscular walls of the heart work nonstop. To do this, they need their own blood supply for nourishment and energy. This comes from arteries that branch over the outside of the heart.

Vena cava

Right atrium

Aorta

Pulmonary artery

Pulmonary vein

Left atrium

Left ventricle

Right ventricle

INSIDE A HEART
Each side of the heart is a two-chambered pump made up of an atrium and a ventricle. Blood flowing from veins enters the small upper chamber, or atrium. It then moves into the large lower chamber, or ventricle, which squeezes it into the arteries.

• THE VITAL SYSTEMS •

From the Heart

Your heart is about the same size as your fist. This bag of muscle filled with blood squeezes tirelessly once every second of your life to pump blood around your body. The heart is made up of two pumps, which lie side by side. The right pump sends blood through the lungs to pick up the vital oxygen needed by all the cells in the body. The left pump sends blood around the body to deliver the oxygen. The blood then returns to the right pump and so on, round and round the double loop of the circulatory system. The heart pushes blood into tubes called arteries, which carry the blood around the body. When the heart relaxes, it fills with blood that comes back from the body along floppy tubes called veins. A heartbeat occurs every time the heart squeezes and relaxes.

OLD HEARTS
Ancient Egyptians believed that the heart was the home of all thoughts, feelings and memories. They placed heart amulets (above) with the dead to help them on their journey to the afterlife.

A HELPING HEART
Some people with heart disease need a new heart. Surgeons are able to remove a healthy heart from someone who has just died and put it into the body of someone who needs it. People of all ages, such as this group (left), have undergone successful heart transplants.

DID YOU KNOW?
When an embryo is four weeks old, its heart starts beating. By the time it is eight weeks old, the heart is fully developed.

10

AT THE HEART OF THE BODY

The heart is in the middle of the chest, slightly to the left side, between the lungs. It is linked into the circulatory system by arteries and veins. About every second, it pumps blood out into the large, strong-walled arteries. These branch around the body carrying blood. The blood flows back along floppy, thin-walled veins, which join together and return it to the heart.

HELPING THE HEART

The heart has valves that make sure the blood flows the correct way. A valve's flexible flaps fold out of the way as blood moves by. If blood tries to flow backwards, the flaps balloon out and their edges slap together, making a seal. This action creates the heartbeat sound. Sometimes a valve may become stiff or weak and will not close properly, causing illness. Faulty valves can be replaced with artificial ones made from metal and plastic (below).

Parts of a
ball-and-cage valve

Moving Things Around

Blood flows from the heart along arteries. These have thick, tough, stretchy walls that withstand the surge of blood pressure with each heartbeat. Arteries divide many times as they spread around the body, and form millions of micro-blood vessels called capillaries. The walls of the capillaries are so thin that vital substances in blood—oxygen, nutrients, high-energy sugars and hormones (chemical messengers)—can seep through to surrounding cells. Carbon dioxide and other wastes from the cells can pass into blood, which takes them away to be removed from the body by the lungs, kidneys and liver. The capillaries join to make larger, thin-walled veins, which return the blood to the heart. Blood carries white cells that fight germs and disease. It also clots to seal leaks and wounds, and it spreads warmth evenly around the body.

A SYSTEM OF BLOOD
Blood flows around the body through veins and arteries. It delivers nutrients, collects wastes and fights germs.

White cell

White cell

INSIDE A CAPILLARY
Blood is made up of plasma, cells and platelets. Plasma is a watery liquid that contains body sugars, salts and many other dissolved substances. There are billions of doughnut-shaped red cells that carry oxygen. Frilly-looking white cells kill germs and clean the blood. Tiny particles called platelets clot blood in wounds.

Red cell

EXCHANGING BLOOD

People have understood for centuries that blood is vital for life. But they did not understand that people have different types of blood. Transfusions were even tried between humans and animals!

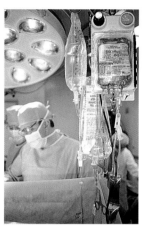

A SAVING DONATION

Donors are always needed to give, or donate, fresh supplies of blood. The blood is transfused into patients who have been injured, or who suffer from blood diseases.

DID YOU KNOW?

A tiny drop of blood the size of a pinhead contains up to 5 million red blood cells, 15,000 white blood cells and 250,000 platelets.

CUT TO CLOT

At a wound, platelets and sticky fibres trap red cells, white cells and germs. A clot is formed that seals the leak.

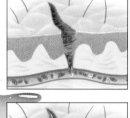

CLOT TO SCAB

Cells at the wound's edges multiply to make new skin as healing begins. The clot hardens into a protective scab.

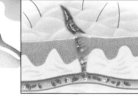

SCAB TO SKIN

Capillaries under the skin reseal, and the new cells grow together. Eventually, the scab falls off and the wound is healed.

BLOOD TYPES

Type A

Each person has a certain type of blood. The main types—A, B, AB or O—depend on proteins called antigens that are in the red cells. Type A blood has antigen A present in the cells and anti-B antibodies in the plasma. Type B blood has antigen B, while type AB has both. A person with type O blood has no antigens in the red cells and both anti-A and anti-B antibodies in the plasma. If a patient receives the wrong blood type, the red cells can fall apart and the blood can clot. Patients must receive blood that matches their own.

Type B

Type AB

Type O

A Deep Breath

You breathe in half a litre (one pint) of air every few seconds when you are resting. The air enters through the nose and mouth, goes down the throat and into the windpipe, called the trachea, before entering the two spongy lungs. The lungs absorb oxygen, which makes up one-fifth of normal air. Oxygen is vital because it is an essential part of the energy-giving chemical reactions inside each cell. The lungs pass the oxygen into the blood, which carries it to all body cells. The body's main waste substance, called carbon dioxide, passes in the opposite direction, from the blood to the air in the lungs. You then breathe this up the windpipe and out—before breathing in new air. The body cannot store much oxygen, so you need to keep breathing to stay alive.

THE DUST REMOVERS
Sticky mucus lines the airways of the nose, throat, windpipe and lungs. It traps dust, dirt and other airborne particles. In the lining of the lungs and windpipe, microscopic hairs called cilia (left) wave to and fro. They push the dirty mucus up to the throat, where it is swallowed.

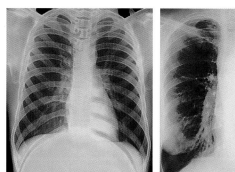
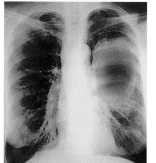

IN THE CLEAR
On an X-ray photograph, healthy lungs (left) show up as faint shapes. Shadowy areas (right) show lungs that have been damaged, for example, by smoking.

DID YOU KNOW?
Each lung contains more than 300 million alveoli, or "air bubbles", which give it a light and spongy texture. The alveoli provide a huge surface area to absorb oxygen. They would cover half a tennis court if they were flattened out.

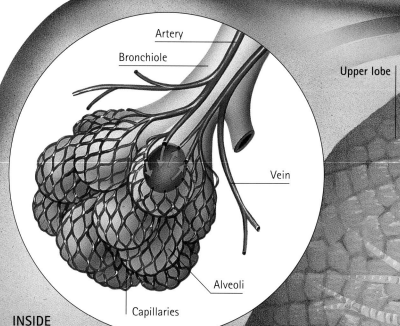

Artery

Bronchiole

Vein

Upper lobe

Alveoli

Capillaries

INSIDE THE LUNGS
In each lung there is a large air tube, called a bronchus, which branches off the trachea. These tubes divide many more times, forming millions of airways called bronchioles. Each bronchiole ends in a cluster of microscopic air chambers, called alveoli, which are surrounded by blood capillaries. Oxygen seeps from the alveoli to the blood in the capillaries.

Lower lobe

Middle lobe

Trachea

INVISIBLE INVADERS

Air may look clean, but it contains all kinds of floating particles, such as dust, pollen grains, bits of animal fur and feathers. Some people are very sensitive to these substances. They sneeze, cough, get runny noses and perhaps attacks of wheezy breathlessness called asthma. Even the powdery droppings of a microscopic creature called the dust mite (right) can float through the air and cause asthma.

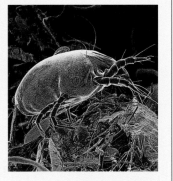

Upper lobe

Pulmonary artery

Pulmonary vein

Bronchus

Diaphragm

Heart

Lower lobe

Nasal cavity

Lung

Diaphragm

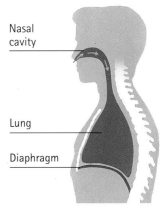

BREATHING IN
The curved diaphragm under the lungs is the main breathing muscle. It contracts and flattens to stretch the lungs and suck in air.

Nasal cavity

Lung

Diaphragm

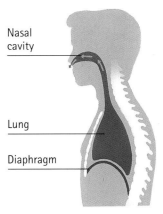

BREATHING OUT
The diaphragm relaxes as we breathe out. The stretched, elastic lungs spring back to their natural smaller size, and blow out air. Rib muscles also help you to breathe.

Discover more in Moving Things Around

EASY TO DIGEST

Salivary glands make watery spit, or saliva. When you eat, the saliva flows into the food and makes it soft and squishy. Saliva also contains enzymes that start to digest food.

Salivary gland

Salivary glands

Open Wide

The food that you eat takes a 24-hour journey through your body. It travels through the digestive tract, a tubelike passage that is about 9 m (29$^1/_2$ ft) long and runs from the mouth to the anus. Food is essential for two main reasons. First, the body needs energy to make it go. Food provides the energy needed to power the millions of chemical reactions that take place in the body. Second, food contains the nutrients needed to make new body tissue and to maintain and replace worn-out cells and tissues. Digestion is the process of breaking down the food, by physical and chemical means, into pieces that are small enough to be absorbed by the body. The mouth is designed to bite off bits of food, mix them with watery saliva, chew them into a soft pulp, and swallow them down the oesophagus into the stomach.

CUTTERS, CHOPPERS AND CHEWERS

Teeth have different shapes and names. The incisors at the front are wide and sharp to cut and bite. The canines are longer and more pointed to tear and rip. The premolars and molars are broader and flatter to chew and crush. There are 32 teeth in a full adult set. On each side of the upper and lower jaw there are two incisors, one canine, two premolars and three molars. The third molars are called wisdom teeth, but many adults do not have all, or any, of these. Children have only 20 teeth in their first full set.

Incisor   Canine   Premolar   Molar

A MOUTHFUL OF FOOD

Each part of the mouth has its own job, but the parts work together as a whole to begin the process of digestion. The lips open to let in food, then seal together to prevent it from falling out. The teeth chop and chew the food while the tongue moves it around. The cheeks bulge as food is squeezed and squashed between the teeth before the tongue presses it into the throat for swallowing.

DOWN IN THE MOUTH
The tonsils are at the very back of the mouth—one on either side. Tonsils are ridges of lymph tissue (left) that help to fight germs and disease. During an infection called tonsillitis, they may swell up with extra fluids, white blood cells and dead germs. If you have tonsillitis, it can be difficult to swallow.

READY
The tongue separates a small portion of the food in the mouth. It presses this against the mouth's roof, or hard palate, to shape it into a soft lump.

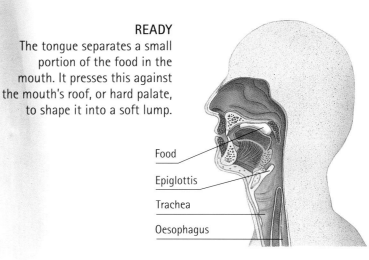

Food

Epiglottis

Trachea

Oesophagus

STEADY
The tongue pushes the lump into the upper throat. A flap, called the epiglottis, closes over the top of the trachea to prevent food from going down it.

Food

Epiglottis

Trachea

Oesophagus

SWALLOW
Muscles in the walls of the lower throat and oesophagus contract in waves. They grasp the lump of food and force it down the oesophagus to the stomach.

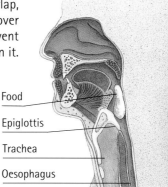

Epiglottis

Oesophagus

Food

Trachea

DID YOU KNOW?
Fresh saliva from healthy salivary glands contains no bacteria or other germs. After chewing, it may contain a million bacteria in one droplet. They come from food and the lining in the mouth.

Discover more in Taste Sensations

JUST SWALLOWED

The stomach's muscular walls squeeze and squirm to mash food (coloured blue). Its lining produces powerful digestive juices that break down food.

AFTER ONE HOUR

Food is turned into a lumpy soup called chyme. Starchy and sugary foods digest fastest, while fatty foods are the slowest.

AFTER FOUR HOURS

The stomach's job is done. The remains exit through the sphincter, which opens regularly to allow squirts of chyme into the small intestine.

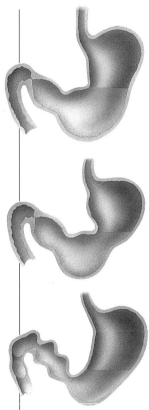

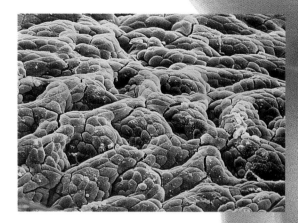

SELF-PROTECTION

The stomach's lining (above) contains tiny glands that make gastric acids, enzymes and mucus. The lining is coated with thick mucus so that it does not digest itself.

Gall bladder

Duodenum

Liver

Large intestine

The Production Line

The first stop for food swallowed down the oesophagus is the stomach. The stomach is the widest part of the digestive tract. It is a muscle-walled bag that can expand to hold about 2 litres (¹/₂ gallon) of food and drink. The stomach breaks up the food with powerful squeezing actions and strong digestive chemicals. The soupy, partly digested food oozes into the next section, called the small intestine. More enzymes are mixed in for further chemical breakdown. The digested nutrients are absorbed into blood flowing through the lining of the small intestine. The large intestine is shorter, but much wider, than the small intestine. Water, body salts and minerals from the undigested food are absorbed here. The brownish, semi-solid remains are called faeces and are stored in the rectum. The final stage is when the remains are passed through the anus.

Appendix

Oesophagus

Stomach

Pancreas

Small intestine

Rectum

FOOD PROCESSORS

The digestive system includes the digestive tract, pancreas, gall bladder and liver. The pancreas and gall bladder empty juices and bile into the small intestine to digest food there. The liver receives digested nutrients in the blood and stores and processes them.

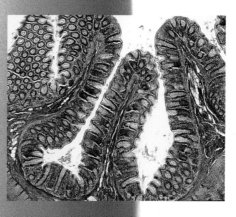

HEALTHY FOODS

To stay healthy, a body needs a wide variety of foods containing important dietary components. These include proteins for growth, maintenance and repair, and starches and sugars for energy. Some fats (especially plant-based ones) make nerves and tissues healthy, but too much fat can harm the heart and blood vessels. Fresh vegetables and fruits provide essential minerals and vitamins, and also fibre, or roughage. This keeps the digestive tract itself healthy and working well.

DID YOU KNOW?

The small intestine is four times longer than the large intestine. The small intestine is an incredible 6 m (20 ft) long while the large intestine is only 1.5 m (5 ft) long.

FRILLY VILLI

The small intestine's velvety lining consists of thousands of finger-shaped villi (left), each about 1 mm ($^1/_{25}$ in) long. They form a huge surface, more than 20 times the body's skin area, to absorb digested nutrients.

The Work Continues

The digestive system is made up of the digestive tract, the pancreas, the gall bladder and the liver. The wedge-shaped pancreas gland, just behind the stomach, makes strong digestive juices to help food digest in the small intestine. The gall bladder is under the liver. It stores bile, a yellowish fluid made by the liver, which also helps digestion in the small intestine. The liver, next to the stomach, is the largest organ inside the body. It has more than 600 different jobs, mostly processing nutrients and other substances that are brought by the blood from the small intestine. After body cells have used their nutrients, they make waste products such as urea. The blood collects the waste products, and the excretory system—the kidneys, ureters, bladder and urethra—gets rid of them as a yellowish fluid called urine.

DID YOU KNOW?

An average adult produces 1,500 ml (45 fl oz) of urine each day. It is 95 per cent water, and 5 per cent wastes such as unwanted salts and minerals. Healthy urine contains no bacteria or other germs.

Liver

Gall bladder

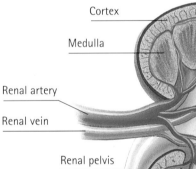

Cortex

Medulla

Renal artery

Renal vein

Renal pelvis

BLOOD'S FILTER
Each kidney's cortex and medulla layers filter blood brought by the renal artery. The filtered blood returns to the heart by the renal vein. Wastes and excess water collect in the renal pelvis as urine.

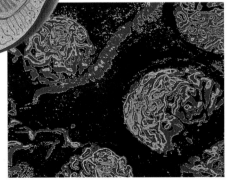

THE EXCRETORY SYSTEM
The two kidneys are in the upper abdomen, just below the liver and stomach. Urine flows to the bladder in the lower abdomen, then out along the urethra.

TINY FILTERS
Each kidney contains about 1 million microscopic blood-filtering units called nephrons (above). Every day, the kidneys filter about 190 litres (42 gallons) of blood.

JUICES FOR DIGESTION
As you eat a meal, the digestive system prepares for action. Bile flows into the small intestine from the gall bladder along the bile duct. It digests mainly fatty foods. Digestive juices flow from the pancreas, along the pancreatic duct, into the small intestine. They digest mainly proteins.

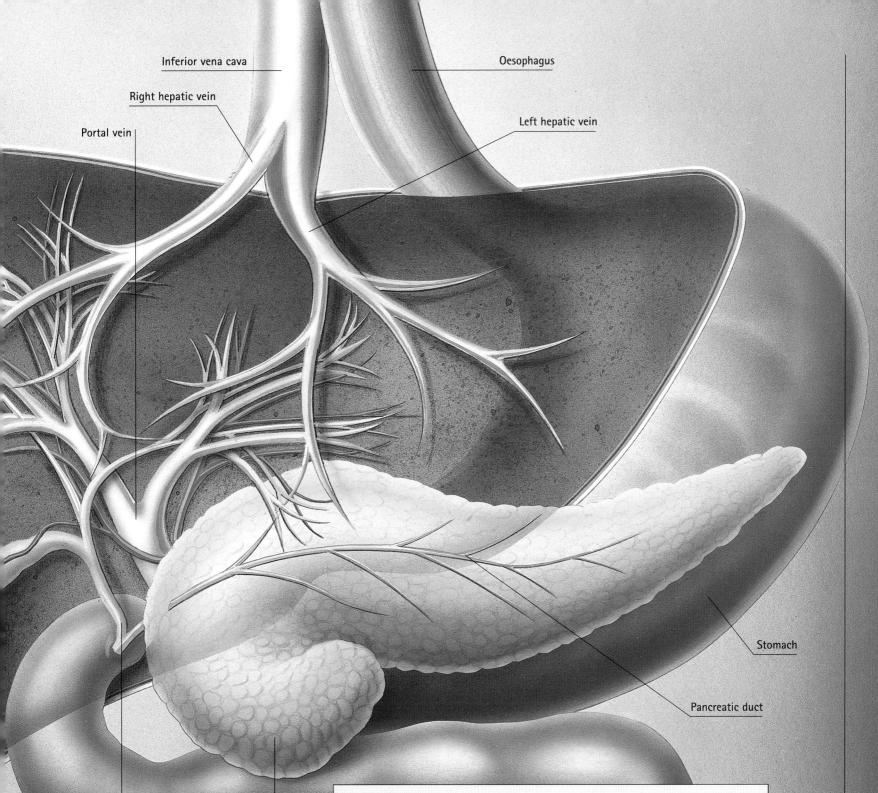

Inferior vena cava

Oesophagus

Right hepatic vein

Left hepatic vein

Portal vein

Stomach

Pancreatic duct

Bile duct

Pancreas

Small intestine

LIFE-SAVING TREATMENTS

Kidneys sometimes become diseased and cannot filter blood. This means that harmful wastes can build up in the body. Sometimes the blood can be filtered through a machine, a renal dialyser, for several hours every few days. Another treatment is to transplant kidneys from a person who has just died, or one from a relative. The kidneys are kept cool and bathed in special fluids (right) before the transplant.

Discover more in The Production Line

21

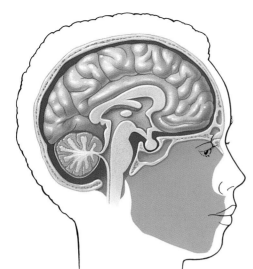

BRAIN PROTECTION
Bones support and protect. The rounded dome of the skull shields the delicate brain from injury. The upper skull, or cranium, is made up of eight curved bones linked firmly at wiggly lines called suture joints.

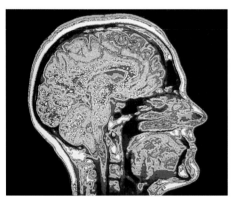

The Bare Bones

Most parts of the body, such as blood vessels, nerves and intestines, are soft and floppy. The whole body can stand up straight and move about because it is held together by a skeleton. This is the inner framework of 206 bones, which are stiff and strong. The skeleton has two main parts. The axial skeleton is the central column, and is made up of the skull, vertebrae (backbones), ribs and sternum. The appendicular skeleton is made up of the bones of the arms and legs. About half of all the body's bones are in the wrists, hands, ankles and feet. Each bone in your body works as a movable beam or lever and is specially shaped to support, protect and withstand stresses and strains. Most bones are linked at flexible joints and pulled by muscles, which allow you to walk, run, jump, and perform more delicate movements.

HEAD BONES
The brain is so securely encased in bone that doctors must use scanners to find out if anything is wrong.

Scapula

Humerus

Ulna

Phalanx

Radius

Suture joints

Skull

Metacarpus

Clavicle

DID YOU KNOW?

The spine, or vertebral column, is made up of 24 vertebrae. These have washer-like discs of flexible cartilage (tough, elastic tissue) between them. As you stand and walk, the body's weight squashes each cartilage disc by as much as 1 cm ($^2/_5$ in) each day. When you lie down, the discs expand to their normal position.

Fibula

Tibia

Femur

Patella

Vertebra

Rib

Pelvis

Sternum

GROWING BONES

Bones grow first as soft, flexible cartilage. This gradually hardens into true bone. It takes many years for some bones to grow, especially those in the wrist and hand. Look at the hand X-rays of a child (left) and adult (right). True bone is the whitest.

BONES, BONES, BONES

Bones are many sizes and shapes. In general, long bones in the limbs are like supporting beams and movable levers. Wide, flat bones in the shoulders and hips anchor many muscles. Each bone has a scientific name, and many have common names, too. The patella, for example, is usually called the kneecap.

AT THE JOINT

Joints, like bones, are designed for their jobs. Joints that allow least movement are the most strong and stable. Suture joints have firmly cemented bones that cannot move. Hinge joints (left) in the knees, elbows and knuckles let the bones move to-and-fro, but not from side to side. Ball-and-socket joints (right) in the hips and shoulders let the bones twist, move to-and-fro, and from side to side. Bones are covered with slippery, shiny cartilage where they meet at the joint. This prevents them from wearing out and keeps the movements of the bones smooth.

Hinge joint

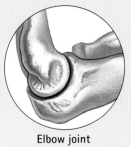
Elbow joint

Ball-and-socket joint

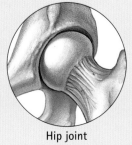
Hip joint

Periosteum

Spongy bone

Compact bone

Bone marrow

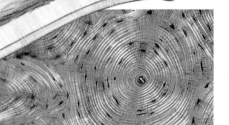

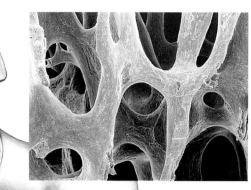

SPONGY BONE
The bone tissue inside the end, or head, of a long bone is called spongy bone (left) because the spaces are filled with fluids and cells. This makes the end light but strong.

COMPACT BONE
A bone is like a tube. The outside is made of compact bone (left) and is hard and dense, while the inside is jelly-like tissue called bone marrow. A living skin, called periosteum, covers the bone.

• THE ULTIMATE STRUCTURE •

What's in a bone?

Bone is living tissue that grows and changes throughout your life. Although bones you may see outside the body are dry and brittle, inside the body, they are one-fifth water and are tough, but flexible. Bone tissue is a mixture of three main substances. One is a meshwork of fibres called collagen, which lets bone bend without snapping. The second is masses of crystals, made up of minerals such as calcium, carbonates and phosphate. These make bone tough and hard. The third is millions of cells called osteoblasts, which build and maintain the collagen and mineral crystals around them. Like other body parts, bones have blood vessels to bring them nutrients and nerves to detect pressure and pain. Bones also respond to change. If you decide to take up weightlifting, for example, your bones will grow new tissue to cope with the new stresses.

A BONE DOME

The human body is a marvellous construction, and designers, architects and engineers have learnt much from it. Just like the human skull, some buildings are dome-shaped. This shape is light, but very strong.

SELF-REPAIR

Bones show up clearly as pale shapes on X-rays, or radiographs. These reveal any break or fracture in the bone. A splint, plaster cast or other support holds the broken bone steady in the correct position so that it can heal itself.

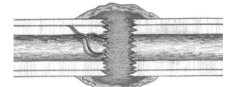

BROKEN BONE

Bones have blood vessels and nerves, so they bleed when broken. The blood clots to seal the leaks.

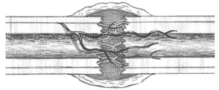

MENDING BONE

Cells at the edge of the break make new hard tissue, which grows into the clot. At first, this is cartilage.

MENDED BONE

The cartilage hardens into true bone. Other cells break up the lumps and "remodel" the bone to its original shape.

RED MARROW, YELLOW MARROW

There are two main kinds of jelly-like marrow in bones. In a baby, most bones contain red marrow, a very busy substance. Each day, red marrow produces millions of new red blood cells, platelets, and some white blood cells, to replace those that die. In adults, red marrow is found in the ends of the long bones, the sternum, ribs, vertebrae and parts of the skull. The other bones contain yellow marrow, which is mainly a store of fats and minerals. Bone-marrow disease may affect the body's disease-fighting immune system, which is based on white blood cells.

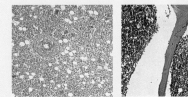

Healthy bone marrow   Sick bone marrow

Muscle Power

PULLING TOGETHER

Many muscles work in pairs. For example, the biceps pulls the forearm bone to bend the elbow. Its opposing partner, the triceps, pulls the other way to straighten the elbow. Muscles must shorten, or contract, to create movement.

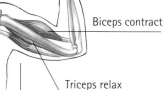

Biceps contract

Triceps relax

Biceps relax

Triceps contract

Every movement you make uses muscles. They allow you to blink, jump, eat, run and sing. Your body has three different kinds of muscles. Cardiac muscle in the heart squeezes life-giving blood around the body. Smooth muscle in the walls of the digestive tract massages food along. The walls of other internal tubes and bags, such as the arteries and lungs, also contain smooth muscle. The most common kind of muscle is skeletal, or striped, muscle. You have about 640 skeletal muscles and these make up two-fifths of your body weight. Some are long, thin and straplike; others bulge in the middle, or are flat and sheet-shaped. Skeletal muscles are joined to bones or to each other. When they contract, they pull on the bones and other tissues, and let you hoist up a huge weight or tie a shoelace.

Trapezius

Deltoid

Hamstring

Gastrocnemius

Triceps

Gluteus maximus

Rectus abdominis

Achilles tendon

DID YOU KNOW?

The biggest muscle in the body is the gluteus maximus, which is in the buttock and upper thigh.
The smallest muscle is the stapedius. This is attached to the tiny stirrup bone, deep in the ear.

LAYERS OF MUSCLES

Dozens of skeletal muscles lie just under the skin. Their narrowed ends form ropelike tendons that anchor them firmly to bones. The muscles crisscross and intertwine to form layers all over the body.

26

MUSCLE POWER

Skeletal muscle has bundles of muscle fibres. They are giant cells, slightly thinner than hairs, up to 30 cm (12 in) long. These muscles are also called striped muscles because they have a regular banded pattern. Smooth muscle has spindle-shaped cells without banded patterns. Cardiac muscle cells branch and rejoin.

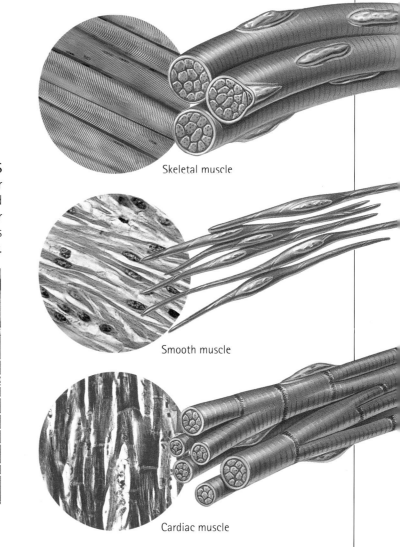

Skeletal muscle

Smooth muscle

Cardiac muscle

FITTER MUSCLES

Exercise makes all your muscles—even the heart and breathing muscles—bigger and more powerful. This makes you feel fit and healthy.

Pectoralis major

Biceps

Digital flexor muscle

MUSCLE PROBLEMS

Muscles that are not used and exercised regularly become weak and floppy. They can shrink and waste away. If your breathing, heart and blood-vessel muscles are weak, you can suffer from health problems. Some diseases affect mainly muscles. Muscular dystrophy is the general name for a group of muscle-wasting diseases. The muscle fibres in people with this disease shrink and die and are replaced by fatty and scar tissues.

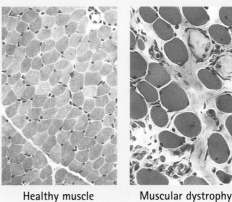

Healthy muscle   Muscular dystrophy

Discover more in On the Move

27

Skin Deep

Skin is the body's largest and heaviest organ. It covers almost 2 sq m (21^1/$_2$ sq ft) on an adult, and weighs up to 4 kg (9 pounds). It varies in thickness from 0.5 mm (^{1}/$_{50}$ in) on the eyelids to 5 mm (^{1}/$_5$ in) on the soles of the feet. Skin keeps in body fluids, salts and soft tissues. It keeps out dirt, germs, water and most harmful rays from the sun. It protects the delicate inner parts of the body against wear and tear, knocks and physical damage, and extremes of temperature. Skin also helps the body to maintain a constant temperature of 37°C (98.6°F). It turns flushed and sweaty to lose extra warmth, or goes pale to save heat. It also provides the body's sense of touch, so that we can detect danger and stay out of harm's way.

ONLY ONE YOU

The ridged patterns of fingertip skin are fingerprints. They help to grip small objects and to identify you. No two fingerprints are the same. The skin replaces itself each month, but fingerprints remain through life.

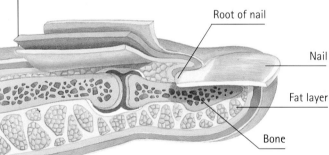

Root of nail

Nail

Fat layer

Bone

AT YOUR FINGERTIPS

A fingernail grows from a fold in the skin at the nail's root. It stays attached along the nail bed. Like a hair, a nail is dead. The nail bed and surrounding skin feel touch and pressure.

LOSING HAIR

Hairs, nails and the tough, dead cells at the skin's surface are all made from a body protein called keratin. An average scalp hair (above) lives for three years before it falls out and is replaced by a new one.

HAIR TYPES

The kind of hair you have depends mainly on its shape. Viewed under a microscope, a cross section of curly hair looks square, wavy hair looks oval and straight hair is circular. Like skin, hair colour is determined by melanin.

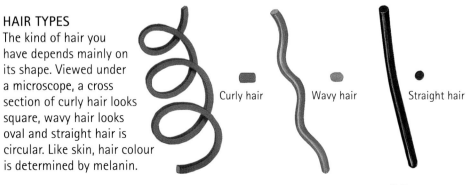

Curly hair

Wavy hair

Straight hair

SEEING INTO SKIN

This close-up of skin shows its two main layers. The epidermis is made of hard, tough cells. A top layer of dead cells rubs off and is replaced by cells multiplying below. The dermis contains many tiny parts such as blood vessels and nerves.

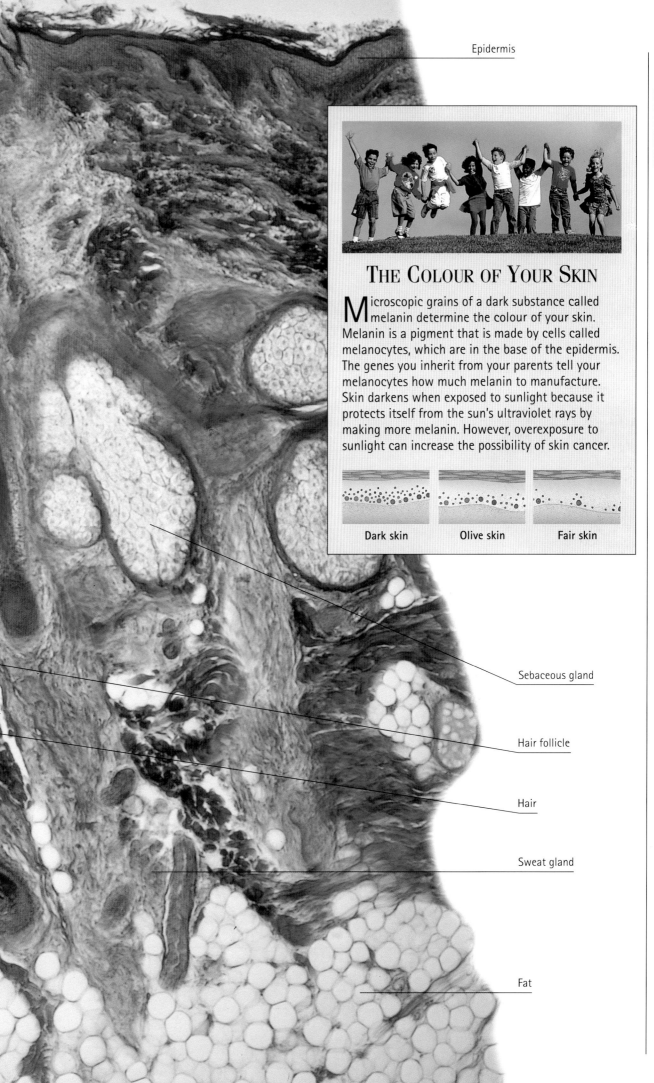

Epidermis

THE COLOUR OF YOUR SKIN

Microscopic grains of a dark substance called melanin determine the colour of your skin. Melanin is a pigment that is made by cells called melanocytes, which are in the base of the epidermis. The genes you inherit from your parents tell your melanocytes how much melanin to manufacture. Skin darkens when exposed to sunlight because it protects itself from the sun's ultraviolet rays by making more melanin. However, overexposure to sunlight can increase the possibility of skin cancer.

Dark skin   Olive skin   Fair skin

Sebaceous gland

Hair follicle

Hair

Sweat gland

Fat

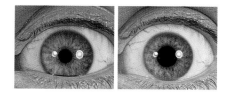

Looking Around

Five main senses tell the body about the outside world: sight, hearing, smell, taste and touch. Sight is the most important. Two-thirds of all the information processed in the human brain comes in through the eyes. Light enters through the clear, domed cornea at the front. It then passes through an adjustable hole, called the pupil, which is situated in a ring of muscle, called the iris. A lens focuses the light rays so that they cast a clear, sharp image on the retina, which lines the back of the eyeball. In the retina, about 130 million light-sensitive cells generate nerve signals when light rays shine on them. Signals are then sent along the optic nerve to the brain. The images formed on the retina are upside down (like those inside a camera), but the brain interprets them the right way up.

BRIGHT AND DIM
The iris adjusts the pupil. The pupil shrinks in bright conditions to keep too much light from damaging the retina (left), and widens in dim conditions to let in as much light as possible (right).

RETINA REVEALED
A doctor or optician sees into the eye with an ophthalmoscope. This shows the retina and blood vessels branching over the eye (left) and gives the doctor valuable information about the eye's health.

Optic nerve

Eye muscle

Retina

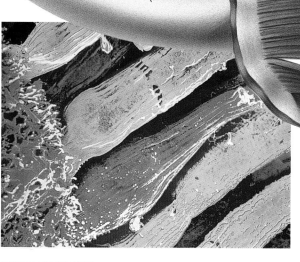

CELLS THAT SEE
The retina has two kinds of light-sensitive cells, called rods (yellow) and cones (blue). Rods work in dim conditions and cannot see colours. Cones can detect colours and fine details, but only function in bright light.

Tear duct

Tear gland

EYE PROBLEMS

Sometimes the eyeball is not the correct shape. If the eyeball is too long, the lens is unable to focus on distant objects and this causes short-sightedness (myopia). If the eyeball is too short, it causes long-sightedness (hyperopia). Glasses or contact lenses are used to correct these problems. If the light-sensitive rods and cones in your retina do not work properly, you can

have problems seeing colours. This can cause confusion between reds and greens. Tests using dots of different colours (left) can reveal colour blindness.

CRYING EYES

Every time you blink, tear fluid is smeared over the eye's surface to wash away dust and germs. The fluid comes from the tear gland, under the upper eyelid. It drains through tear ducts into the nose. This is why crying makes you sniff.

Sclera

Pupil

LOOKING INSIDE

The main part of the eyeball is filled with a clear, jelly-like fluid, called vitreous humour. It keeps the eye firm and well shaped. The sclera is the eye's "white", its tough outer covering. Eye muscles behind the eyeball move it within its bony socket in the skull.

Iris

Cornea

Lens

DID YOU KNOW?

The human eye has been a powerful symbol for many cultures through the centuries. Many people believed that dreadful things, such as disease or death, could happen if someone was looked at with the evil eye. Today, some cultures still paint eyes on their fishing boats to ward off the bad luck of evil eyes.

Discover more in The Control Centre

Listening In

Eyes see light, but they cannot see sound. Sound travels as invisible waves of high and low air pressure and is detected by your ears. The outer ear funnels these waves into the ear canal. They bounce off the eardrum, a small flap of taut skin, and make it vibrate. The eardrum is joined to a tiny bone called the hammer. The vibrations pass by the hammer, and two other miniature bones, the anvil and stirrup. After passing through a flexible membrane called the oval window, the vibrations move into a snail-shaped, fluid-filled area called the cochlea. Ripples are created in the cochlea's fluid. The ripples move microscopic hairs that stick out from rows of hair cells in the fluid. The hairs' movements generate nerve signals that pass along the auditory nerve to the brain.

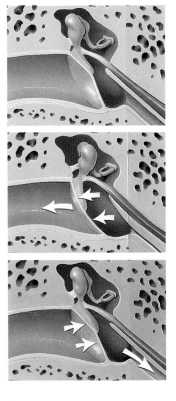

EQUAL PRESSURE
The middle-ear chamber is a tiny air pocket behind the eardrum. The Eustachian tube links it to the throat, and so to outside air.

PRESSURE UP
The outside air pressure is less when you are up high. Because the middle-ear pressure stays the same, the eardrum bulges and your hearing fades.

PRESSURE DOWN
If you swallow hard, the Eustachian tube opens. Air rushes out of the middle ear to relieve the pressure. Your eardrum "pops" back to normal.

EYES AND EARS
The ear canal of the outer ear is 3 cm (1⅕ in) long. This means the delicate hearing parts of the middle and inner ear are set deep in the head, almost behind the eye. They are well protected inside the thick skull bone.

Human: 20–20,000

Dog: 15–50,000

Bat: 1,000–120,000

Vibrations per second (Hz)

0   100   1,000   10,000   100,000

HEARING SILENCE
The pitch or frequency of sound, from low to high, is measured in vibrations per second, or hertz (Hz). Human ears hear about 20 to 20,000 Hz, but animals can hear even higher pitched, or ultrasonic, sounds.

INSIDE THE EAR
The outer ear is large and obvious and guides sound waves into the ear canal. Three tiny ear bones vibrate in the air-filled middle-ear chamber, which is set into the skull bone. The snail-shaped cochlea converts vibrations to nerve signals.

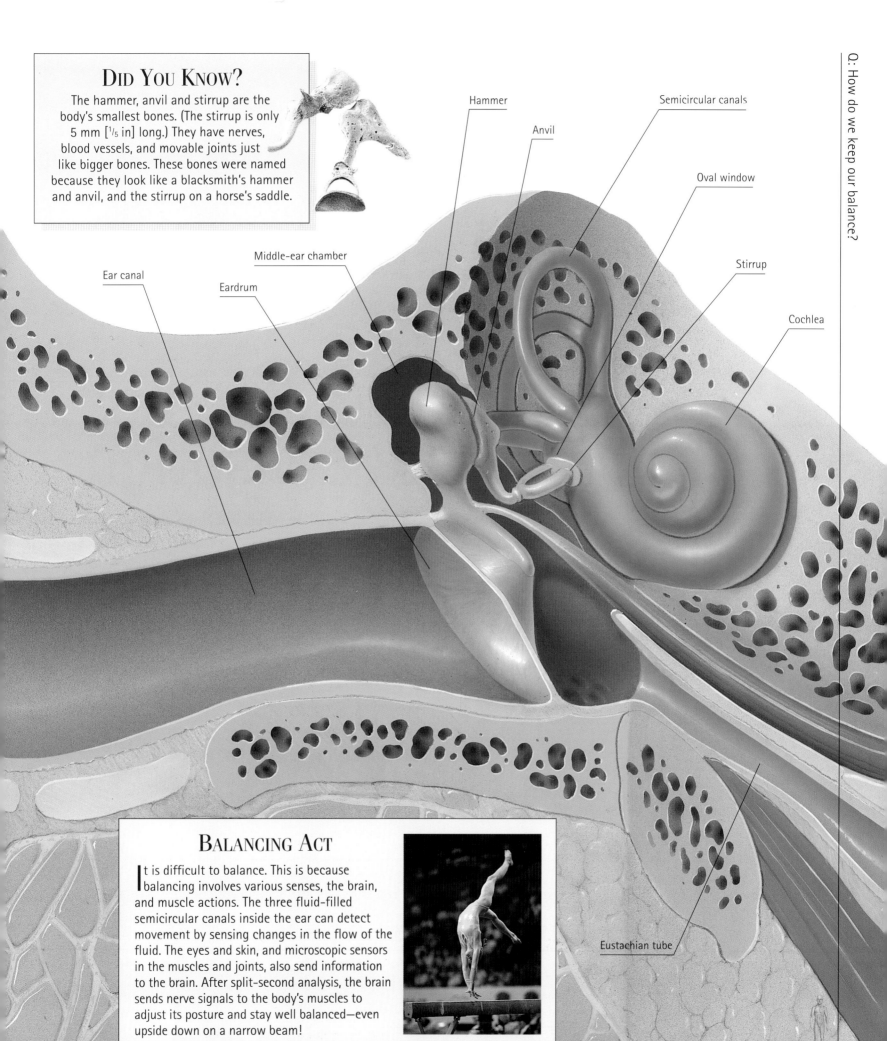

DID YOU KNOW?

The hammer, anvil and stirrup are the body's smallest bones. (The stirrup is only 5 mm [1/5 in] long.) They have nerves, blood vessels, and movable joints just like bigger bones. These bones were named because they look like a blacksmith's hammer and anvil, and the stirrup on a horse's saddle.

Hammer

Semicircular canals

Anvil

Oval window

Middle-ear chamber

Stirrup

Ear canal

Eardrum

Cochlea

BALANCING ACT

It is difficult to balance. This is because balancing involves various senses, the brain, and muscle actions. The three fluid-filled semicircular canals inside the ear can detect movement by sensing changes in the flow of the fluid. The eyes and skin, and microscopic sensors in the muscles and joints, also send information to the brain. After split-second analysis, the brain sends nerve signals to the body's muscles to adjust its posture and stay well balanced—even upside down on a narrow beam!

Eustachian tube

Discover more in Communication

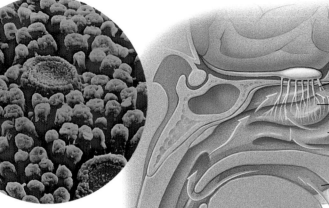

Olfactory nerves

Olfactory area

Nasal cavity

Oral cavity

Pharynx

ON THE TIP OF THE TONGUE
The tongue has small lumps and bumps, called papillae, which help to grip food. The much smaller taste buds are set into the surface around their edges.

A GOOD SNIFF
When you breathe normally, air flows into the nasal cavity. To smell or sniff, air swirls around the ridged bones in the nose up to the olfactory areas in the nasal cavity's roof.

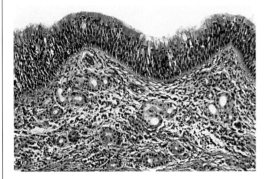

HAIRS THAT SMELL
Each olfactory area has 10 million cells that detect chemicals. Each cell has a tuft of up to 20 long hairs, called cilia. Different smells settle on these hairs and trigger nerve signals. An average person can identify 10,000 different smells.

• FROM THE OUTSIDE WORLD •

Taste Sensations

Taste and smell work in similar ways. They are both chemosenses, which means they respond to certain chemical substances. Taste detects flavours in food and drink. As you chew, watery saliva dissolves the flavours from foods. These flavours are picked up by more than 8,000 taste buds in the tongue's upper surface. Each taste bud has up to 50 chemical-sensing cells clustered together like segments of an orange. Smell detects odours floating in the air. The different odours around you land on two thumbnail-sized patches inside the top of the nose, called the olfactory areas. Taste and smell can help to warn you if food or drink is bad. They also detect delicious aromas and flavours. Smell alone can also warn you of danger, such as smoke from a fire.

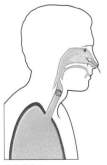

AAAAA...
You sneeze when dust, animal fur or plant pollen irritates the sensitive lining of the nose.

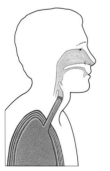

AAAAA...
The throat and windpipe close. Muscles in the chest and abdomen press the lungs and squash the air inside.

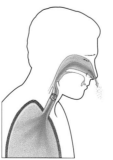

CHOOO!
When the windpipe and throat open again, high-pressure air blasts through the nose to blow away the irritants.

TASTES ON THE BRAIN
When the tongue's taste buds detect certain flavours, they send nerve signals along sensory nerves to the taste centres in the brain. These sort the signals and identify the taste. Smell signals run from the olfactory areas in the top of the nose to the olfactory bulb. This sorts out some of the smells and passes the signals on to the olfactory centres in the brain.

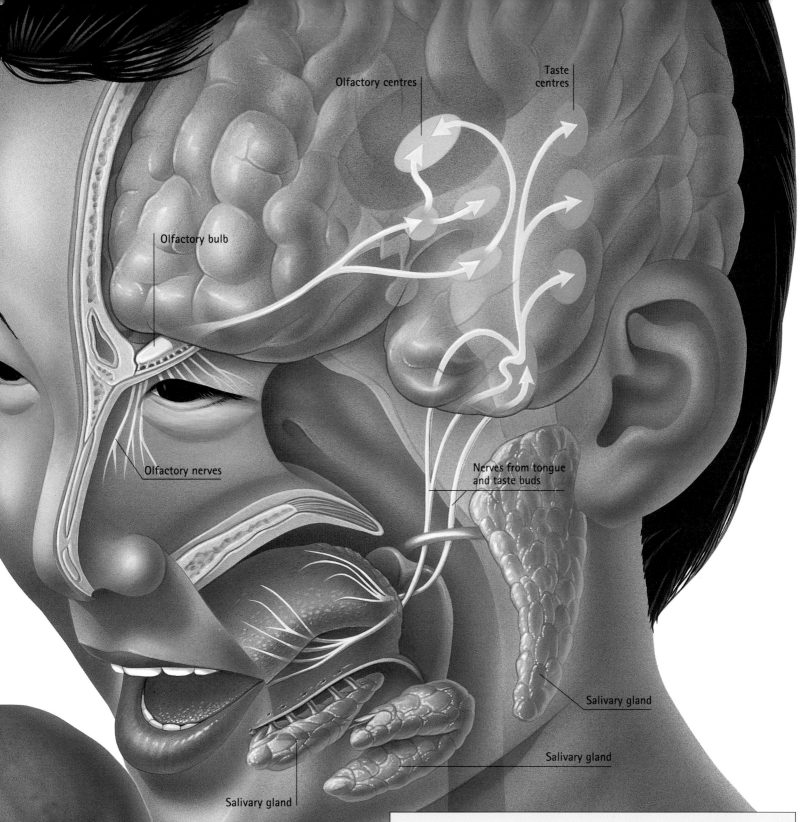

Olfactory centres

Taste centres

Olfactory bulb

Olfactory nerves

Nerves from tongue and taste buds

Salivary gland

Salivary gland

Salivary gland

FOUR FLAVOURS

Hundreds of different tastes, from chocolate to lemon, are combinations of four basic flavours: bitter, sweet, sour and salty. Different parts of the tongue sense different flavours. Touch sensors inside the mouth detect pressure, hardness, texture, heat and cold. Although smell and taste are separate senses, the brain adds together their information. "Taste" is really a complicated combination of taste, touch, temperature and smell.

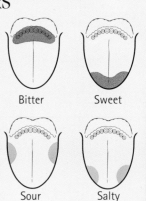

Bitter

Sweet

Sour

Salty

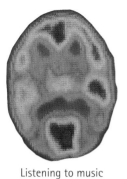

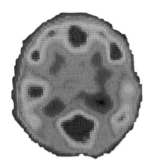

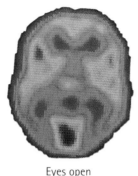

Listening to music   Understanding language   Eyes closed   Eyes open

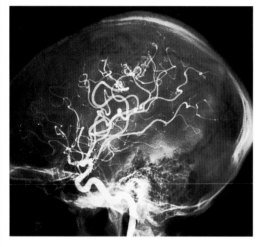

BRAIN'S BLOOD SUPPLY
An angiogram X-ray (above) shows arteries bringing blood to the brain. These angiograms can help to identify problems, such as strokes and brain tumours. If the blood supply to the brain stops for more than just a few minutes, parts of the brain begin to die.

• TOTAL CONTROL •

The Control Centre

The brain is the control centre of the body. All the nerve signals from the eyes, ears and other sense organs travel to the brain to be sorted and analysed. These signals tell the brain about conditions outside the body. The brain decides what to do, and sends nerve signals to the muscles that control body movements. There are also sensors inside the body that send nerve signals to the brain, telling it about body conditions such as temperature, blood pressure, and amounts of oxygen, carbon dioxide, nutrients and fluids. The brain automatically controls breathing, heartbeat, digestion and many other inner processes. When nutrients or fluids run low, your brain makes you feel hungry or thirsty. The brain is the place where you think, remember, work out problems, have feelings, imagine and daydream.

DID YOU KNOW?

The brain is one-fiftieth of the weight of the whole body, but it consumes one-fifth of all the energy used by the body. This means the brain is ten times more energy-hungry than any other body part. Whether you are thinking or fast asleep, your brain is using energy constantly.

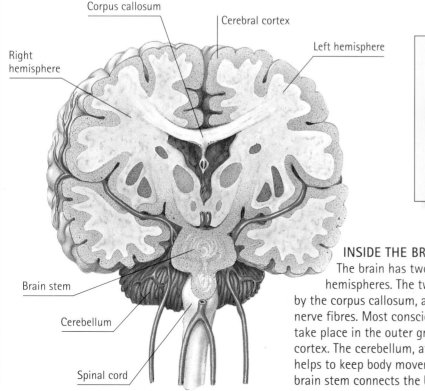

Corpus callosum

Cerebral cortex

Right hemisphere

Left hemisphere

Brain stem

Cerebellum

Spinal cord

INSIDE THE BRAIN
The brain has two parts called cerebral hemispheres. The two hemispheres are linked by the corpus callosum, a bridge of 100 million nerve fibres. Most conscious thoughts and feelings take place in the outer grey layer, called the cerebral cortex. The cerebellum, at the rear of the brain, helps to keep body movements coordinated. The brain stem connects the brain to the spinal cord.

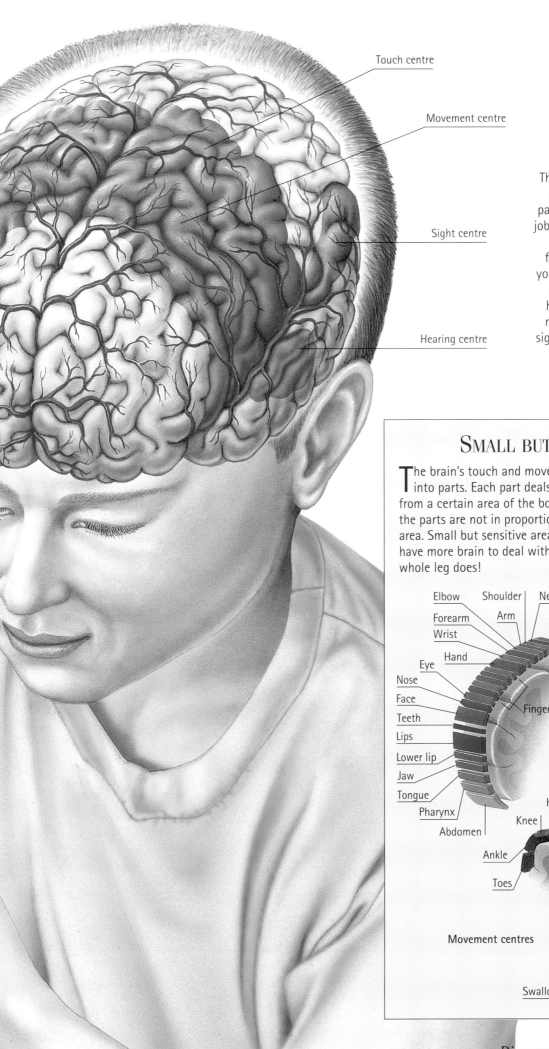

Touch centre

Movement centre

Sight centre

Hearing centre

BRAIN CENTRES

The cerebral cortex looks the same all over, but different parts, or centres, do different jobs. The sight centre receives and analyses nerve signals from the eyes. This is where you really "see". Other senses, such as hearing and touch, have their own centres. The movement centre sends out signals to the body's muscles.

SMALL BUT COMPLEX

The brain's touch and movement centres are divided into parts. Each part deals with nerve signals coming from a certain area of the body, such as the lips. But the parts are not in proportion to the size of the body area. Small but sensitive areas, such as the lips, can have more brain to deal with their signals than a whole leg does!

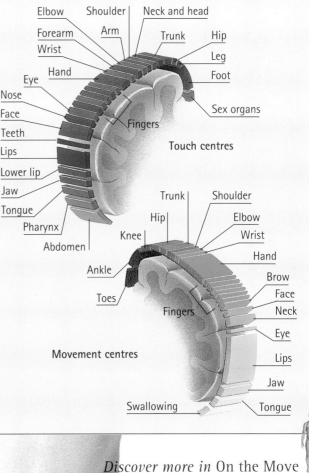

Elbow   Shoulder   Neck and head
Forearm   Arm   Trunk   Hip
Wrist   Leg
Hand   Foot
Eye
Nose
Face   Sex organs
Teeth   Fingers
Lips   **Touch centres**
Lower lip
Jaw
Tongue
Pharynx
Abdomen

Trunk   Shoulder
Hip   Elbow
Knee   Wrist
Ankle   Hand
Toes   Brow
Fingers   Face
Neck
Eye
Lips
Jaw
Movement centres
Swallowing   Tongue

Discover more in On the Move

HOT FOOT

Long ago, people believed that nerves were tubes of fluid flowing to and from the brain. They thought this fluid carried messages around the body. If you burnt your foot, for example, the fluid told your brain to pull your leg away.

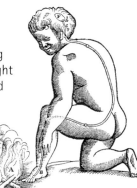

DID YOU KNOW?

If you sit in an awkward position, the nerves are sometimes squashed and blood vessels cannot supply vital nutrients and oxygen. A part of your body may "go to sleep", or feel numb. When you change your position, the pressure is relieved, blood flows, and the nerves begin to work again.

What a Nerve!

The brain is not isolated in its curved casket of skull bones. It is linked to all parts of the body by nerves. Nerves are long, pale and thin, like pieces of shiny string. The main nerve is the spinal cord, a bundle of millions of nerve cells with long, wirelike fibres. The spinal cord is about 45 cm (18 in) long, and is as thick as an index finger. Branches of nerves connect it to the skin, muscles and other body parts, and the upper end merges with the brain. The lower end tapers into a stringy cord inside the vertebrae (backbones) of the lower back. The billions of nerve cells in the brain, spinal cord and nerves are linked into a vast web, or network, which carries tiny electrical nerve signals.

NEURAL NETWORK

Each nerve cell has spidery dendrites that gather signals from other nerve cells at synapses. The signals travel along the cell's main wirelike section, called the axon, before passing on to other nerve cells.

Nerve cell body

Synaptic cleft

Axon

Synapse

Dendrite

JUMPING THE GAP

Nerve cells link together at trillions of junctions called synapses, but they do not touch. They are separated by a tiny gap called the synaptic cleft. Nerve signals cross this gap as chemicals, called neurotransmitters, before continuing in an electrical form.

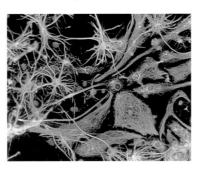

THE FLEXIBLE TUNNEL

A tunnel formed by holes in the vertebrae protects the spinal cord from knocks and kinks. Like the brain, the spinal cord is wrapped in three cushioning layers, or membranes, called the meninges. Thirty-one pairs of nerves branch out from the spinal cord to other areas of the body.

QUICKER THAN THINKING

Sometimes your body reacts quickly, before you even think about it, to avoid harm or danger. If a ball comes near your head, you close your eyes, turn your head and throw up your hands. These quick, automatic reactions are called reflexes. Sometimes the brain is not involved in reflexes. If your fingers accidentally get too hot, the skin sends nerve signals to the spinal cord, which sends other signals straight back to your arm muscles, and you pull your hand away. This is called the withdrawal reflex.

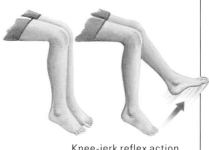

Knee-jerk reflex action

Withdrawal reflex

Vertebra

Spinal cord

Nerve

Intervertebral disc

MOTHER'S MILK
The pituitary "master gland" produces six main hormones. One is called oxytocin. This releases milk from a mother's breast.

FATHER'S BEARD
The male hormone testosterone comes from a man's testicles. It produces certain body features such as a deep voice and facial hair.

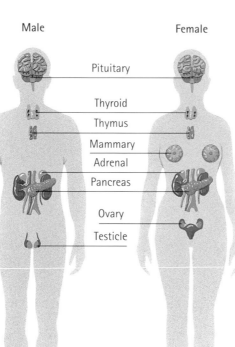

Male

Female

Pituitary
Thyroid
Thymus
Mammary
Adrenal
Pancreas
Ovary
Testicle

HORMONE-MAKING GLANDS
These are the main endocrine, or hormone-making, glands. The kidneys, stomach, intestines, heart and other organs make their own hormones.

CALCIUM CONTROL
The thyroid gland in the neck has four pea-sized parathyroid glands, which make parathormone. This hormone controls the levels of the mineral calcium (above) in bones and blood.

FLIGHT, FIGHT OR FRIGHT!
A roller-coaster ride makes your heart race, blood pressure rise, breath shorten, muscles tense and pupils widen. The hormone adrenalin, made by the adrenal glands above the kidneys, causes these effects. They are known as the "fight or flight" reaction because the body decides whether to face danger or flee from it.

• TOTAL CONTROL •

The Activators

The body is controlled by different systems. The brain and nerves send electrical signals through the body very quickly. The endocrine system works more slowly using chemicals called hormones. This system helps to regulate the amounts of nutrients, fluids and minerals. It activates and controls long-term growth, from baby to adult. The endocrine glands make more than 50 different hormones. Each hormone circulates in the blood and affects the workings of certain areas, such as organs and tissues. The thyroid gland produces thyroxine, which controls how quickly cells use energy. The thymus gland makes hormones that help white blood cells defend the body against disease. The adrenal glands make hormones that regulate sodium and other minerals, and help the body cope with stress and disease. The pea-sized pituitary gland just beneath the brain controls and coordinates the whole endocrine system and links it to the brain and nerves.

40

MISSING HORMONES

The two main jobs of the pancreas are to make digestive juices and hormones. In some people, the pancreas cannot make the hormone insulin, which controls the amount of energy-giving glucose in the blood. The resulting condition, called diabetes mellitus, can lead to serious illness. Injections of artificially produced insulin replace the missing natural insulin.

ON THE BOIL

A boil is a small-scale or localised area of inflammation, usually due to infection with germs. The germs, white cells and fluids gather in a hair follicle and make it swollen and tender—and fit to burst!

THE BATTLE RAGES

If germs get into the blood and multiply, they cause infection throughout the body. A high temperature is one sign of the body's reaction to invasion.

GERM INJECTION

A mosquito's needle-like mouthparts slide through human skin to suck blood, and inject any germs picked up from previous victims.

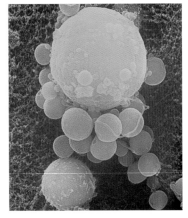

KILLERS ON THE LOOSE

White blood cells called T-cells control many features of immune defence. Other cells called killer T-cells (left) destroy invading germs on contact.

• WORKING TOGETHER •

Under Attack

The body is always under attack. Microscopic germs such as bacteria and viruses float through the air, enter skin cuts, and settle on food and drink. The body has many defences. Tough skin keeps out many would-be invaders. They are trapped and killed by slimy mucus and natural chemicals in the linings of the nose, mouth, throat, lungs and gut. But if germs get in, the body also has internal defences. The immune system, based on white blood cells called lymphocytes, makes substances known as antibodies. These stick to and destroy any germs that invade the body. The body also reacts to infection by a process known as inflammation. The infected part swells and becomes red, hot and sore, as white blood cells of many kinds rush to tackle the problem.

EATEN ALIVE

Large white blood cells, called macrophages, crawl through blood and tissues to gather at the battle site in their millions. They search for germs, bits of body cells and other debris, which they surround and engulf. One macrophage (below) can "eat" more than 100 invading bacteria.

STRANGE BUT TRUE

There are complex links between the brain and the immune system. Some people believe that they will become very sick if a medicine man (above) places a curse on them.

ALL-ROUND PROTECTION

A pale fluid called lymph flows around the body through its own system of lymph vessels and nodes (glands). This system delivers nutrients, collects wastes and removes germs.

WHEN DEFENCES ARE DOWN

Human Immunodeficiency Virus (HIV) attacks parts of the immune system that are meant to protect the body against germs. It destroys particular white blood cells called helper T-cells. As the body loses its defences, after months or years, HIV can lead to the general condition known as Acquired Immune Deficiency Syndrome (AIDS). The body is then open to other diseases, such as infections like pneumonia and types of cancers.

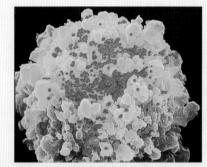

HIV-infected cell

SILENT SPEECH

Some people who cannot hear and have difficulty learning to speak use sign language. Their hand and finger positions can convey letters, letter groups, words, phrases and other information (left).

LETTERS AND WORDS

There are more than 2,000 different written languages. Most of these have an alphabet of basic units called letters, which are combined into groups known as words. Here are just some of the ways the words "the human body" can be written.

⠙⠮ ⠎⠊⠇⠑⠝⠞ ⠎⠏⠑⠑⠉⠓
Braille

ΤΟ ΑΝΘΡΩΠΙΝΟΝ ΣΩΜΑ
Greek

ТЕЛО ЧЕЛОВЕКА
Russian

人體
Chinese

• WORKING TOGETHER •

Communication

Humans communicate with each other every day using sounds and body movements. Most commonly, we share information about the world around us through spoken languages. These are special sounds we make to represent objects, actions, numbers, colours and other features. We use our brains to remember words, put them in the correct order, and make the larynx, or voice box, produce the correct sounds. If a person is unable to speak, he or she can communicate in other ways, often by using sign language. We also have written and pictorial languages, which are signs, symbols and squiggles that represent spoken words. The whole body works together to help us convey our innermost thoughts and feelings through language.

SHAPING SOUNDS

The jaws, tongue, cheeks and lips help to shape sounds, such as words, from the larynx. But not all the sounds from the larynx are words. They can be laughter, sad sobs or screams of pain.

Aaah

Eeee

Oooh

Mmmm

SOUNDS OF SPEECH

The sounds we make come from the larynx at the top of the trachea. It has two vocal cords at its sides. Air passes silently through the wide gap when we breathe normally. When we speak, the muscles pull the cords close together. Air then flows up the trachea making the vocal cords vibrate to produce sounds.

Larynx

Vocal cords

Trachea

GETTING AROUND
Some people cannot move around easily because they have an injury, a disease or a disability. Wheelchairs and other devices help them to move more freely and to take part in sports.

IN THE SWIM
A dolphin swishes its broad tail with powerful back muscles to surge through the water at high speed. Humans can also swim underwater, but they need the help of diving equipment to stay underwater for long periods.

On the Move

Your body is constantly on the move. Even when you are resting or sleeping, oxygen, nutrients and other chemicals spread throughout the body, and cells grow, multiply and migrate. The heart pumps blood, lungs breathe and food squeezes through your stomach. When you are awake, your body is also in continuous motion—from glancing quickly to jumping in the air. The body's inner parts work together for movement. The brain sends signals along nerves to muscles, telling them to contract. The muscles need the oxygen and energy-rich sugars that are brought by blood, which is pumped by the heart. The lungs absorb oxygen, while the intestines digest nutrients from food. All of this happens in animals, too. Many animals are built for specialised movements—whales can swim, bats can fly and monkeys can climb. But the human body is probably the best all-rounder. People can do many things and they use their brains to invent special equipment to allow them to do even more.

ON THE RUN
A cheetah can run faster than any other animal. With four long, slim legs and a flexible body, it is built for speed. Humans can run short and long distances, but they are never as fast as the cheetah.

IN THE SKY

Birds can fly because they have extra-light bodies and powerful chest and shoulder muscles. Humans need to use equipment, such as a hang-glider, to fly.

UP THE SLOPE

Sloths hang around in trees all day, and all night, too. Their hooklike claws are made for climbing. Humans can climb, but they often need to use picks, ropes and other equipment.

SLEEPING ON THE JOB

Scientists study people to find out what happens when we sleep. They have discovered that the body slows down, and the skeletal muscles are relaxed and still. But the body is still moving and working. The heart

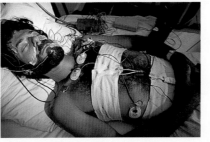

pumps blood, lungs breathe air, intestines digest food, kidneys make urine, and millions of electrical signals fly around the brain. Sleep is vital and a person without it will die sooner than a person without food. By the time you are 60, you will have spent 20 years sleeping.

Discover more in Growing Up

47

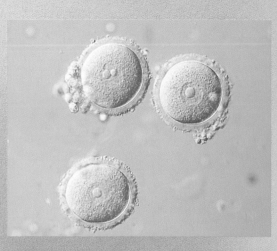

A MASSIVE CELL

The ripe egg is one of the largest cells in the human body. It is full of nutrients for the early stages of a baby's development. Like the sperm, the egg has only a half-set of DNA.

FEMALE PARTS

Each month one ovum, or egg, ripens and passes along the Fallopian tube to the uterus, or womb. The womb lining becomes thick and rich in blood to nourish the fertilised egg as it develops. If the egg is not fertilised, the womb lining is not needed. It breaks down and comes away through the vagina as fluids and blood. This is called menstruation.

Fallopian tube

Uterus

Ovum

Ovary

Bladder

Position of female reproductive system

Urethra

Vagina

How Life Begins

The body has systems for digestion, movement and other activities. It also has a system for reproduction. The reproductive system is different in men and women. The parts of the female system are inside the lower abdomen. Glands called ovaries contain egg cells, or ova. The main parts of the male system are just below the lower abdomen. Glands called testicles contain sperm cells, or spermatozoa. Together, one egg and one sperm contain all the information and instructions necessary to create life. The instructions are in the form of genes, which are made from the chemical deoxyribonucleic acid (DNA). When a sperm fertilises an egg, a baby begins to develop in the woman's womb.

DID YOU KNOW?

An enormous set of instructions—between 100,000 and 200,000 genes—is needed to create a human body.

ANCIENT ART

People have always known that babies grew in a mother's uterus, or womb. The ancient Egyptians used hieroglyphs, or picture-symbols, such as these to represent the uterus.

COILS AND SUPERCOILS

Every cell contains DNA molecules. These hold all the genetic information, such as height and hair colour, that makes you different from every other living thing. A DNA molecule is made up of four chemicals that fit together to form what look like the rungs of a twisting ladder. As a DNA molecule becomes tightly coiled, it forms part of a threadlike object called a chromosome. A sperm and an egg usually have 23 chromosomes each, a half-set of DNA. When they join, every cell in the new human body has 46 chromosomes, a full DNA set.

MALE PARTS
The testicles, or testes, contain cells that continually divide to form millions of sperm cells every day. The sperm are stored in a coiled tube called the epididymis. During sexual intercourse, sperm are forced along the vas deferens and then along the urethra by powerful muscular contractions. About 400 million sperm come out of the urethra in a milky fluid called semen.

SEEING THE INVISIBLE
People could not see sperm or egg cells until the microscope was invented. Dutchman Anton van Leeuwenhoek made his own microscopes, such as the one below, and drew the first published pictures of sperm (left) in 1677.

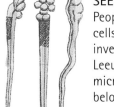

Position of male reproductive system

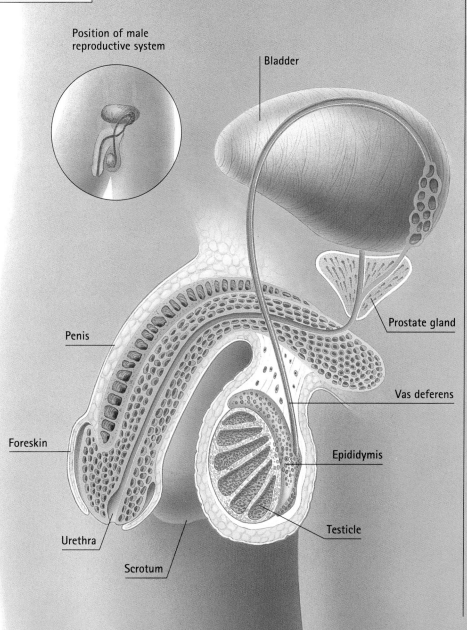

Bladder

Prostate gland

Penis

Vas deferens

Foreskin

Epididymis

Urethra

Testicle

Scrotum

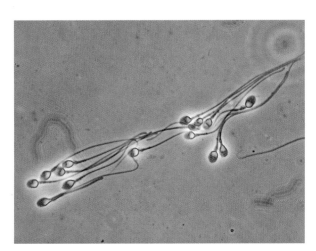

TINY SWIMMERS
Sperm cells are like microscopic tadpoles that swim by lashing their tails. The half-set of DNA that they carry is inside the front end, or head, of the sperm.

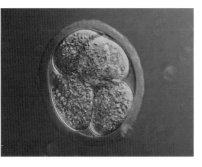

THE SPERM MEETS THE EGG

Hundreds of sperm cells gather around the egg cell as it moves slowly along the Fallopian tube to the uterus. But only one sperm will merge with, or fertilise, the egg.

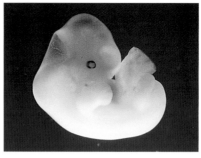

THE CELLS DIVIDE

The fertilised egg divides into two cells. These split into four cells, then eight, and so on. After a few days, there is a ball of dozens of cells.

AN EMBRYO FORMS

Four weeks after fertilisation, cells are multiplying in their millions and forming tissues and organs, such as the brain, the liver and the heart, which has already started to beat.

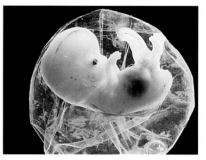

THE BODY SHAPES ITSELF

Six weeks after fertilisation, the grape-sized embryo begins to develop arms and legs. The head is bigger than the body and has eyes and ears.

• FROM THE BEGINNING •

Early Life

When the egg and sperm join at fertilisation, they form a single cell that is smaller than the head of a pin. The cell divides into a ball of cells that burrows into the blood-rich womb lining, absorbs the nutrients there and starts to grow. This time is called gestation, or pregnancy. From about the fifth month, the mother can feel the foetus kicking and moving about in the bulging uterus. The foetus floats in a pool of fluid, protected and cushioned from knocks and noises. It cannot breathe air or eat food. It obtains oxygen and nutrients from its mother's blood through an organ the size of a dinner plate, called the placenta, which is in the wall of the uterus. The foetus is linked to the placenta by a curly lifeline called the umbilical cord, through which blood flows. Nine months after fertilisation, the foetus has developed into a baby who is an average of 50 cm (19^1/$_2$ in) long and 3.4 kg (7^1/$_2$ lb) in weight.

DID YOU KNOW?

A baby has more than 350 bones in its body. Some of these gradually join together during childhood to form the 206 bones of an adult skeleton.

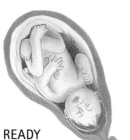

READY FOR BIRTH

The powerful muscles in the walls of the uterus contract during labour. They begin to push the fully developed baby into the birth canal.

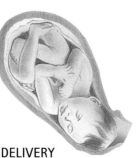

DELIVERY

The baby's head, its widest part, passes through the cervix, or opening of the womb. It emerges from the birth canal.

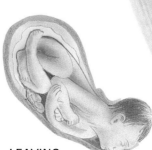

LEAVING THE WOMB

The muscles of the uterus continue to contract. The baby slips from warmth and darkness into the outside world.

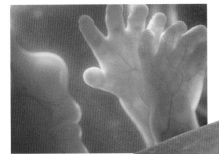

THE FOETUS FORMS

Eight weeks after the sperm joined the egg, the embryo is as big as a thumb and looks human. All major parts and organs have formed, and it is now called a foetus.

SIX MONTHS TO GO

The foetus is about 6 cm (2¹/₃ in) long. It hiccups and moves its arms and legs as it floats in the watery amniotic fluid inside the womb. In the final months, the foetus grows eyelashes and nails and becomes much larger.

DIFFERENT GENES

Each human body has a unique set of genes. Identical twins, however, develop from a fertilised egg that has split into two. Each half then develops into a complete human being. The twins look the same because they have identical genes. Fraternal twins develop together but each comes from a separate egg and sperm. Because their genes are different, they do not look the same.

51

TALL AND SMALL
People who have an excess of the growth hormone grow too much, while those with too little do not grow enough. Doctors can now treat these conditions to help people grow to a normal size.

Growing Up

The body grows by increasing its cell numbers. Growth is fastest in the mother's womb, and continues very rapidly during the first two years. Then, it begins to slow. Growth is controlled mainly by a growth hormone that is made by the pea-sized pituitary gland below the brain. Sex hormones control physical changes when girls are between 10 and 14 years old and boys are between 12 and 14 years old. A girl develops breasts, rounded hips and other female features. A boy develops a deep voice, facial hair and other male features. The body's final height is due largely to the genes inherited from the parents. However, the human body also needs nutrients, energy and raw materials from healthy food to grow properly. As the body develops, so does the mind. We learn how to communicate and perform hundreds of other day-to-day tasks.

David, age 2 years

ON YOUR FEET
Children grow fastest in their first two years of life. By the age of two, most children can walk and run.

HAND OVER HAND
By the age of seven, children can perform delicate tasks with their hands. They have begun to develop independent thought.

FOR THE FIRST TIME
By the time babies are eight months old, they have learnt to move their arms and legs and to sit up. They have also grown teeth.

David, age 6 months

David, age 7 years

GROWING OLDER

The average human body peaks in size and physical fitness at about 20 years of age. The body begins to age after this, but for many years the ageing process can hardly be noticed. Gradually the ageing signs become more obvious. Hair turns grey, skin becomes wrinkled, reactions become slower, muscle strength decreases, height reduces, senses lose their sharpness, and even memory and concentration become less efficient. However, these signs happen at very different ages and rates in each individual.

Sam, age 4

Sam, age 6

Sam, age 8

SELF-PORTRAITS

Some skills combine your physical and mental abilities. To draw, you have to be able to use a pen or a brush. This involves your brain, nerves and hand muscles and feedback from your eyes. But you also show your understanding and experience of the world in your drawings.

David, age 10 years

MENTAL NOTES

At about the age of ten, a child's growth rate once again increases. The child's mental development is very important at this age.

THE CHANGING YEARS

At 12–14, everyday activities are usually mastered. The body goes through puberty and grows very quickly.

David, age 13 years

David, age 18 years

GROWN UP

At 18–20 years of age, the average person is physically fully grown and is considered adult.

Spare Parts

Most parts of the body can be replaced by an artificial part called a prosthesis. This is a substitute for a natural body part that did not develop properly or was damaged by an injury or disease. Some prostheses, such as myoelectric hands, do the missing parts' job. Others, such as false eyes, may improve the body's overall appearance. Prostheses can also provide framework and support for the remaining natural parts. A metal plate, for example, can repair a broken bone. Artificial parts that are put into the body, such as metal joints or heart valves, are called implants. Natural body parts that are transferred between bodies, or different parts of the body, are called transplants. Skin is transplanted from one part of the body to another, but organs such as hearts and kidneys are often transplanted from someone who has just died.

A METAL PUMP
Disease may cause the heart to pump at an irregular rate, or to stop pumping altogether. Today, specialists are developing pumps like this to help the heart pump.

FROM THE HIP
This artificial hip joint copies the original ball-and-socket design, with a steel ball on a spike in the thigh bone, and a plastic socket cemented to the hip bone. It can replace a hip joint that has become stiff and painful through a disease such as arthritis.

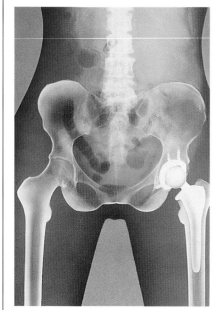

A CLEAR VIEW
Some people wear contact lenses instead of glasses. These help the eyes' own lenses, and are less noticeable than glasses.

PLASTIC EYES
Some people have diseases of the eyes. Sometimes their eyeball or eyeballs may be removed to prevent a disease from spreading. Modern plastic eyes look very real, but the wearer cannot see with them.

LOUD AND CLEAR
Electronic engineers have developed a cochlear implant (left) for the part of the inner ear that changes sound vibrations into tiny electrical nerve signals. This implant allows some deaf people to hear again.

ELECTRIC HANDS
The myoelectric hand has an electric motor that moves its fingers and can grip even small, soft objects. Its metal wires and sensors detect signals in nearby nerves and muscles, so the wearer can control it precisely.

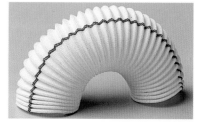

A NEW ARTERY
Special tubing (above) can replace diseased or damaged arteries. The inner surface of the tube is coated to prevent blood from sticking to it or clotting in it.

Glass eye

Rigid wooden leg

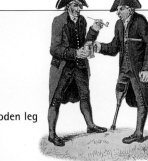

BODY BUILDING

For centuries, people have used the technology and materials available to them to build spare parts for the body and alter its appearance. False teeth have been made from many different materials, including wood, ivory and even gold! Eyes of glass were created to replace eyes that were lost through injury or disease. Rigid artificial arms and legs were made from wood. As engineering techniques improved, flexible limbs with hinges, levers and even wheels inside were built. Wigs have often been worn to cover baldness, but they have also been used as fashion accessories!

Flexible wooden arm

17th-century wig

A HELPING MACHINE

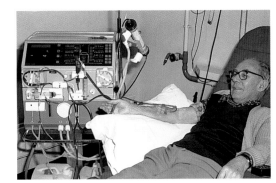

Sometimes machines help the human body to function properly. When a person's kidneys are diseased, the renal (kidney) dialysis machine filters and cleans their blood. Tubes carry the patient's blood to the machine and back again. Most patients need dialysis for several hours, several times a week.

SECOND SKIN

Surgeons are able to reuse skin from many areas of the body to help heal or replace skin that has been damaged or diseased in other areas. Specialists have also developed artificial skin, which allows the real skin underneath to heal naturally.

HI-TECH LEG

The modern artificial leg has a hinged knee joint and a realistic-looking foot. It is a great advance on the wooden peg leg worn by some pirates hundreds of years ago.

A FALSE BITE

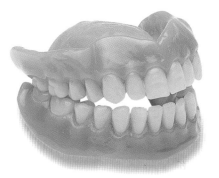

Dental engineers use the hardest types of modern plastics and composites for modern false teeth, or dentures.

Index

Picture Credits

(t=top, b=bottom, l=left, r=right, c=centre, F=front, C=cover, B=back, Bg=background)
Ad-Libitum, 31tr, 44bc, 54br, 54c, 55bl (S. Bowey), 11br (Royal North Shore Hospital, Sydney/S. Bowey), 55tcl (Sydney Artificial Eyes/S. Bowey). AKG, London, 7tl (Naturhistorisches Museum, Vienna/E. Lessing). Auscape, 47cr (E. & P. Bauer), 46c (Ferrero/Labat), 43tc (S. Wilby & C. Ciantar). Austral International, 10bl (T. Bauer), 42tc (H. Pfletschinger/ Camera Press), 46tl (Rex Features), 55bc (Sipa-Press/F. Durand), 54tr (Sygma/I. Wyman). Australian Picture Library, 38tl (Bettman), 46cl, 47tl (Minden Pictures), 29tr (West Stock). Biophoto Associates, 27tcr, 30tr, 50tr. The Bodleian Library, Oxford, 6tl (MS. Ashmole 399, fol. 19r, 20r). The Bridgeman Art Library, 55tcr (Christie's, London), 55tr (London Library, St. James's Square), 8tl (Museum of the History of Science, Oxford). The British Museum, 10cl. Cochlear Ltd, Australia, 54cr. The Granger Collection, 6tr, 7tr, 50cl. Sally Greenhill, 44tl. The Image Bank, 31bc (D. de Lossy), 40tr (C. Navajas). Image Select/Ann Ronan, 49bcl, 49cl. International Photo Library, 42tr (Superstock). John Watney Photo Library, 25tc. Mary Evans Picture Library, 9tr, 55tl. Medical Images, Inc, 13tcl (B. Slaven), 20bc (H. Sochurek). Melbourne Muscular Dystrophy Association of Victoria (Neurology Department, Royal Children's Hospital), 27br. Lennart Nilsson, 50/51c. Otto Bock, 55r. Peter Arnold, Inc, 45tr (L. Dwight), 54bl (Siu). Petit Format, 52bc, 52bl, 52br, 53bc, 53bl, 53br (A. Chaumat), 51tl (Guigoz). The Photo Library, Sydney, 23cr (Biophoto Associates), 41br (M. Clarke/SPL), 24tcl (J. Durham/ SPL), 8bcl (GJLP-CNRI/SPL), 13tr, 52tl (Hulton Deutsch), 25bc (A. Kage/SPL), 39tc (N. Kedersha/SPL), 27c (M. King), 30bl (B. Longcore), 16tl (J. Mazziotta/ SPL), 19br, 34cl (H. Michler/SPL), 19tr (J. Mills), 50tcr (P. Motta & S. Makabe/ SPL), 14cl, 18tc, 24tc (P. Motta/SPL), 43br (NIBSC/SPL), 40cl (A. Pasieka/SPL), 36tc (M. Phelps & J. Mazziotta/SPL), 50tl (D. Phillips), 54cl (Photo Researchers, Inc/C. Bjornberg), 55c (C. Priest/ SPL), 15tr, 28c (D. Scharf/SPL), 10tl, 14bl, 25br, 33tc, 42cl (SPL), 28/29c (S. Terry/SPL), 54tcr (TSI/Med. Illus. SBHA), 25tl, 50tcl. Photo Researchers, Inc, 27bcr, 27tr (M. Abbey/Science Source), 36cl (S. Camazine/B. Camazine), 8bl (Dept. of Energy), 17tr (K. Eward/Science Source), 53tl (F. Grehan), 34tl (Omikron), 30cl (D. Wong). Rainbow, 51br (C. Dittmann), 45tc, 47bc (D. McCoy), 21br (H. Morgan), 8tcl (B. Stanton). The Science & Society Picture Library, 6bl (The Science Museum). Sport The Library, 33bc (D. McNamara). Stock Photos, 42/43c (D. Kunkel/Phototake), 40tl (Mug Shots), 8cl, 22cl (The Stock Market/H. Sochurek). Dr. John Tyler, 48tl, 49bl.

Illustration Credits

Susanna Addario, 3, 5tr, 16bl, 16tc, 17cr, 28cl, 28bc, 29cr. Sam Burgess, 53tr. Dr Levent Efe/CMI, 5tc, 12bl, 13cr, 16br. Christer Eriksson, 12/13c, 16/17c, 40/41c. John Foerster/Foerster Illustration, Inc, 10/11c, 10tr, 44/45c. Chris Forsey, 8/9c. Adam Hook/ Bernard Thornton Artists, UK, 6/7c. Janet Jones, 4bc, 24/25c, 24tl, 25cr. R. Spencer Phippen, 32/33c, 32cl, 32bl, 32c. Trevor Ruth, 4tl, 5cr, 14/15c, 15cr, 38/39b, 39bl, 39tl, 39cr, 46/47c. Christine Shafner/K.E. Sweeney Illustration, 23bc, 23br, 26cl. Kate Sweeney/K.E. Sweeney Illustration, 1, 4cl, 22/23c, 22tl, 23tl, 26/27c, 27cr, 30/31c, 30bc, 31tl, 34tc, 34bl, 35c, 35br. Rod Westblade, 2, 18/19c, 18tl, 20/21c, 20bl, 20c, 37br, 40c, 42tl, 43tr, 48cl, 48bl, 48br, 49cr, 49c, 49tl, 50b, endpapers, icons. Steve Weston/Linden Artists, 36/37c, 36bl.

Cover Credits

John Foerster/Foerster Illustration, Inc, FCcl. Janet Jones, FCtr. The Photo Library, Sydney, Bg (P. Motta/SPL). Kate Sweeney/K.E. Sweeney Illustration, FCc. Rod Westblade, BCtl, BCtr.